50 easy recipes for cooking with beer

Lachlan Anderson

50 easy recipes for cooking with beer

COOKBOOK

50 easy recipes for cooking with beer

Copyright © 2020

Lachlan Anderson

All rights reserved. No part of this book may be transmitted, copied, duplicated without the written consent of the author.

Publisher: Absolute Author Publishing House

Library of Congress Cataloging-in-Publication Data

50 easy recipes for cooking with beer/Lachlan Anderson

p. cm.

ISBN: 978-1-64953-046-2

TABLE OF CONTENTS

FOREWORD 7
APPETIZERS & BREAD 8
    BEER BACON BREAD 9
    HONEY BEER BREAD 10
    BAKED BEER MUSHROOM SOUP 12
    SPICY PARMESAN CHIPS 14
    WALNUT POTATO NUT BREAD WITH BEER 15
    PEARS - BEER - MUSTARD 17
    MEXICAN TURKEY CHILI WITH BEER 18
    FLAT CAKES MADE QUICKLY WITH BEER WITHOUT YEAST 20
    BAKED BREAD WITH BEER 21
    ANDI'S BREAD CHIPS (BONUS) 22
    WHITE BREAD WITH BEER 23
    PUMPKIN - BEER - SOUP 25
MAIN COURSES 27
    ROAST PORK WITH BEER 28
    ROAST PORK IN ONION - BEER SAUCE 30
    BEER MUSTARD MARINADE FOR STEAKS 32
    AMERICAN BEER HAMBURGERS BUN 34
    BRATWURST WITH ONION-BEER SAUCE 36
    UNKELER BEER STEW 38
    BEER GARLIC CHICKEN 40
    BRATWURST BRAISED IN BEER 42
    BRATWURST GOULASH WITH BEER 44
    BRAISED MEAT WITH BEER 46
    SPARE RIBS BASED 48
    CHICKEN IN PLUM BEER SAUCE 50
    IRISH SHEPHERD'S PIE WITH BEER 52
    CHICKEN BRAISED IN BEER AND ONION SAUCE 55

BEER MUSTARD SLICED	57
BEER - CHICKEN	59
MASTER BREWER'S DISH WITH BEER	61
BEER MUSTARD GRILL MARINADE	63
LENTIL SOUP WITH BEER AND BACON	64
BEEF SIRLOIN IN MUSTARD	66
ACHIMS BEER AND POTATO GRATIN	68
BRAISED PORK GOULASH WITH BEER	70
CUCUMBERS IN BEER	72
BEER PASTA SALAD	74
BRAISED CHICORY IN BEER	76
BEER ROOT VEGETABLES	78
BEEF HIP STEAK WITH ONION BEER SAUCE	80
CHEESE BEER TART	82
BEER CHILLI	84
BEER POTATO GRATIN	86
VEGAN GOULASH WITH BEER	88
SPARE RIBS WITH BEER	90
BREWERY GOULASH	92
FLETCHER'S BEER ROASTER	94
VEGAN COFFEE COCOA BEER CHILLI	96
ROAST BEEF WITH BEER	98
DESSERTS	**100**
BEER CREAM SLICES	101
MINI BRIOCHES WITH BEER AND CARAMEL SAUCE	103
BEER - ICE CREAM	105
MORE BOOKS FROM LACHLAN ANDERSON	**106**
Coorie Cooking: Scottish Recipes To Warm Your Heart And Heal Your Soul	106
Coorie: What You Need to Know About The Scottish Lifestyle Trend	106
The Coorie Adult Coloring Book	107
TO FINISH	**108**

FOREWORD

While translating (into German) my book of recipes from my home country, Scotland, during these hot summer nights I often had a beer to go with the work. This led me to the idea of publishing a book with my favourite beer recipes. So, I started, and faster than I thought it came to the end, while my German translation is still "under construction". I hope you enjoy this one with beer in the meantime!

The recipes are easy to follow and I liked them all!

Thanks to my wife for here patience during these summer evenings with my computer time. You're the best wife of all!

Enjoy!

Lachlan

APPETIZERS & BREAD

BEER BACON BREAD

Ingredients for 3 portions

500 g   Flour

1 pack   Baking powder

2 teaspoon   Sea-salt

½ litre   Beer, dark

250 g   Bacon

Preparation

Total time about 1 hour

Preheat the oven to 200 degrees top and bottom heat and grease a tin or bread tin.

Leave the bacon in the pan and let cool. Mix the flour with baking powder, salt and the beer. Then fold in the crispy bacon. Fill the dough into the mould and bake for about 45 minutes.

HONEY BEER BREAD

Ingredients for 1 bread

12 g	Yeast
1 tbsp	Honey
250 g	Wheat flour (whole grain)
250 g	Water
150 g	Rye flour
500 g	Flour
4 teaspoon	Honey
100 g	Water
150 g	Beer (Bitburger works best)
15 g	Salt

Preparation

Total time about 13 hours 15 minutes

Mix the ingredients for the pre-batter and let it stand for 12-24 hours.

Knead the batter with the remaining ingredients slowly for 5 minutes, then let it rest for 30 minutes, take the dough out of the bowl and fold, fold, fold, then shape into a ball and let it rest for another 10 minutes.

Pull together, roll in flour, twirl and tie a knot. Let go for 1 hour.

Baking times:

250 ° C 15 minutes

BAKED BEER MUSHROOM SOUP

Ingredients for 4 portions

500 ml	Beer, light (Pilsner tastes best)
250 g	Mushrooms of your choice, fresh
120 g	Bacon
2	Onion
4 disc	Puff pastry approx. 50 g each
200 g	Creme fraiche Cheese
1	Egg yolk
1 bunch	Parsley
Salt and pepper	
10 g	Butter

Preparation

Total time about 30 minutes

Clean the mushrooms and dice them. Peel onions and dice together with the bacon.

First fry the bacon in the melted butter, then add the onions and mushrooms. Do not let it brown and deglaze with beer. Chop parsley and add. Mix in crème fraiche. Season with salt and pepper and let simmer for 5 minutes.

Pour into fireproof soup cups brush the edges of the cups with whisked egg yolk. Roll out the puff pastry and cut out circles the size of the soup cups. Place them on the soup cups and press them on the edge. Brush again with egg yolk.

SPICY PARMESAN CHIPS

Ingredients for 1 portion

200 g   Parmesan

3   Chili pepper, dried

1 teaspoon   Fennel seeds

Preparation

Total time about 10 minutes

Preheat the oven to 200 degrees (top / bottom heat). Line two baking sheets with baking paper.

Very fine mortar the fennel seeds and the chilli. Grate the parmesan. Put a heap of one level teaspoon of Parmesan on the tray. Press with a spoon to cookies - should be very thin. Pour some of the chilli-fennel mixture over it.

Place in the oven at 200 degrees for 5 minutes. In the meantime, prepare the second sheet. When the sheet comes out of the oven, wait a short while and then remove the chips with a pallet.

WALNUT POTATO NUT BREAD WITH BEER

Ingredients for 2 portions

200 g	Rye flour, dark
350 g	Wheat flour
500 g	Potato
1	Carrot, grated
2 Tea spoons	Salt
1 handful	Hazelnuts
1 handful	Walnuts, chopped
1 handful	linseed
1 handful	Sunflower seeds
½ cube	Yeast, fresh
1	Egg
100 ml	Water
100 ml	Beer

1 tbsp	White wine vinegar
Something	Salt water for brushing

Preparation

Total time about 3 hours 10 minutes

Boil the potatoes and peel them and peel them. Mix the types of flour together and mix in the nuts and salt. Dissolve the yeast in the water.

Press the potatoes into the flour with a potato press. Add the yeast-water mixture, the beer, the vinegar, the egg and a grated carrot to the flour and knead everything into a smooth dough (if necessary, use more flour or add a little water if the dough is too dry). Cover and let the dough rise in a warm place for about 1 hour until the volume has doubled.

Shape the dough into a loaf of bread, place it on a baking sheet lined with baking paper and let it rise again for 1/2 - 1 hour. Cut the loaf in a cross shape and at approx. 40 min at 220 ° C (top / bottom heat) to bake.

PEARS - BEER - MUSTARD

Ingredients for 2 portions

2m	Beer
400 g	Pears, peeled, diced finely
40 g	Mustard seeds
1½ teaspoon	Sugar
¾ TL	Spice mix (pear bread spice)
1 teaspoon	Salt
100 g	Mustard, milder
1 teaspoon	Vinegar (white wine vinegar)

Preparation

Total time about 20 minutes

Put all ingredients up to and including salt in a pan and bring to the boil, cover and simmer over medium heat for about 20 minutes. Place the pear-beer mixture with the remaining ingredients in a tall container, mash them finely.

MEXICAN TURKEY CHILI WITH BEER

Ingredients for 4 portions

1	Hot peppers, red
	Salt and pepper
600 g	Turkey breast
3 teaspoon	Oil
1 package	Vegetables (Mexican pan vegetables), frozen, 650 g
200 ml	Beer
1 teaspoon	Chives, finely chopped
3	Garlic cloves

Preparation

Total time about 20 minutes

Cut the pepper into small cubes. Cut the turkey meat into approx. 2 cm cubes and season with salt and pepper.

Fry the meat well in oil, lift it out of the pan and set aside. Heat the vegetables in the roast residue, add the beer and bring to the boil. Add the turkey meat, hot peppers and chopped or crushed garlic and simmer on a low flame for about 8 minutes. Don't forget to stir!

Stir in the chives before serving.

Serve with rice or white bread as a side dish.

FLAT CAKES MADE QUICKLY WITH BEER WITHOUT YEAST

Ingredients for 1 portion

250 g	Flour
130 ml	Beer
30 ml	Water
Something	Salt and pepper
N.B	Olive oil for brushing
	Herbs, Italian

Preparation

Total time about 17 minutes

Knead the flour, beer and water together, pushing the dough several times with your thumb so that air can get in. Divide the dough into 4 portions, roll it out very thinly round, brush with olive oil, pepper, salt and sprinkle thinly with the Italian herbs.

Bake on baking paper at 220 ° C (top / bottom heat) for about 7 - 10 minutes. Tastes best with tzatziki.

BAKED BREAD WITH BEER

Ingredients for 1 portion

600 g	Flour
500 ml	Malt beer, or other beer
1 bag	Baking powder
2 Tea spoons	Salt
1½ cup	Sunflower seeds, or other, such as roasted onions

Preparation

Total time about 1 hour

Mix all the ingredients together and form the dough into a loaf. Sprinkle sunflower seeds on top and some water.

Bake in the oven at 200 degrees for 55 minutes. Place a cup of water next to it.

If you bake in the Ultra from Tupper, you can omit the cup of water. Then bake for 35 minutes with the lid on and 15 minutes without the lid on.

ANDI'S BREAD CHIPS (BONUS)

Ingredients for 2 portions

200 g	Bread - leftovers, stale
125 g	Herb butter
75 g	Butter
2 Tea spoons	Spice mix, (butter bread salt)

Preparation

Total time about 35 minutes

Cut the bread into thin slices.

Melt the butter and herb butter and add the butter bread salt, Put bread slices in the butter and wait until they are completely soaked.

Spread on a baking sheet lined with baking paper and bake at 180 ° for approx. 12-15 minutes in hot air until it has a nice brown color.

Let cool and enjoy.

By the way: Ok, this one isn't with beer but it's such an easy one and always useful to make something of older bread, that I thought I add it nonetheless.

WHITE BREAD WITH BEER

Ingredients for 1 portion

1,100 g	Flour
1 cube	Yeast
2 Tea spoons	Salt
3 teaspoon	Sugar
7 teaspoon	Oil
1	bottle Beer
50 ml	Milk, lukewarm

Preparation

Total time about 1 hour 20 minutes

Put the milk in a large bowl, add the sugar and yeast and mix everything until the yeast has dissolved. Let stand for about 10 minutes. Then add the flour, salt oil and beer and knead well with a dough hook or a food processor.

The dough must now be left to rise in a warm place for about 30 minutes, it is best to cover the bowl with a dish towel. Then knead the dough again briefly and let it rise again for about 30 minutes.

Then divide the dough in half and put them in a box shape (lightly greased). However, it can also be done directly on the baking sheet, without a mould, just like the baking sheet with baking paper.

Bake the bread at 175 ° C for 30 to 35 minutes.

PUMPKIN - BEER - SOUP

Ingredients for 4 portions

2	Shallots
30 g	Clarified butter
400 g	Pumpkin meat
2 teaspoon	Vinegar (white wine vinegar)
1 liter	Beef broth
Salt and pepper	
Something	sugar
1 bottle	Beer (pilsner)
125 ml	Whipped cream
Cress	

Preparation

Total time about 30 minutes

Finely dice the shallots and sweat them quickly in hot fat. Add the diced pumpkin, deglaze with vinegar, pour broth and cook until soft. Pass the whole thing, season with salt, pepper and sugar. Fill up with the beer, heat again, whip the cream and fold in. Sprinkle with cress and serve immediately.

MAIN COURSES

ROAST PORK WITH BEER

Ingredients for 4 portions

1 kg	Roast pork
1 small Bottles	Beer
2 disc	Bread (mixed bread)
1 large	Onion, cut into small pieces
1 teaspoon	Mugwort
Salt	
Pepper	
Caraway seed	

Preparation

Total time about 30 minutes

Rub the meat with salt and pepper and brown it in hot fat.

Then add the bread slices or edges and the finely chopped onion to the roast and lightly brown. Then add a little cumin and mugwort.

The whole thing is now poured over with beer and braised slightly covered.

After about 30 minutes, pour the sauce stock over the roast and add some water if necessary.

Cook the meat covered.

Bread makes binding the sauce unnecessary.

The amount of beer, caraway and mugwort can vary depending on your taste.

ROAST PORK IN ONION - BEER SAUCE

Ingredients for 6 portions

2 kg   Roast pork with rind

1 kg   Onion, cut into fine half rings

2 tbsp   Oil

Salt

Pepper

Nutmeg

500 ml Beer (pilsner)

Preparation

Total time about 45 minutes

Cut the rind into a diamond shape. Soak the rind (not the meat) for 2 hours. Pat the meat dry, salt (especially between the cuts) and pepper. Sear in oil from all sides in an ovenproof roaster, just not on the rind. Take the meat out of the roasting pan. Braise the half onion rings in the meat fat until they are slightly golden yellow. Put the meat on top with the rind on top. Put in the preheated oven to 200 ° C and pour in a little Pils (do not pour over the meat in the first half hour otherwise it will not be crispy. Pour a total of 0.5 l of Pils over time. The roast must remain in the oven for about 2.5

hours. After half an hour, reduce the temperature to 180 ° C. Always water the meat, otherwise it will dry. After the cooking time, remove the meat from the roaster, let something rest. Puree the sauce with the magic wand, possibly extend with a little water if it is too thick. Season with salt, pepper, possibly a little nutmeg

BEER MUSTARD MARINADE FOR STEAKS

Ingredients for 4 portions

4	Steak (s), e.g. pork neck / comb steaks)
½ liter	Beer, pilsner or dark
1 large	Onion
2 toes	Garlic
	Mustard medium hot

Salt and pepper

Preparation

Total time about 6 hours 25 minutes

Peel the onion and cut it into coarse rings. Roughly chop the cloves of garlic. Wash the steaks, pat dry, salt, pepper and spread mustard on both sides. Then layer the meat, the onion rings and the garlic in a Tupper tin, baking dish or similar. Pour beer over it so that everything floats in it. Cover and let infuse for approx. 6 hours.

Remove the steaks from the marinade for grilling. The onion rings can be grilled in a piece of aluminum foil.

AMERICAN BEER HAMBURGERS BUN

Ingredients for 12 portions

1,350 g	Minced beef, lean,
2 m.	Onion, finely chopped
9	Clove of garlic, finely chopped
3 teaspoon	Worcestershire sauce
1 teaspoon	Salt
1 teaspoon	Pepper, black
180 ml	beer
235 ml	Milk
120 ml	Water
55 g	Butter, soft
560 g	Flour
1 pack	Dry yeast

2 tbsp	Sugar, whiter
1	Egg

Preparation

Total time about 1 hour 52 minutes

Hamburg buns should be prepared first, then burgers. Heat milk, water and butter together to approx. 35 - 40 ° C. Mix half of the flour, yeast, sugar and salt in a large bowl, add the milk mixture and then the egg. Then stir in the remaining flour.

When all the ingredients have combined well, lift the dough out of the bowl and knead well on a floured board until the dough is nice and elastic, this takes about 8 minutes.

Now divide the dough into 12 pieces of equal size, shape into balls and place on a greased baking sheet. Press a little flat. Cover and let go for 30 - 35 minutes.

Preheat the oven to 200 ° C (top / bottom heat). Bake the buns for 12 minutes until golden brown. Take out of the oven and let cool until lukewarm.

Meanwhile prepare the burgers. Prepare the grill and oil the grillage slightly. However, the burgers can also be fried in a pan.

Mix the ground beef, onion, garlic, Worcestershire sauce, salt and pepper well in a bowl. Add the beer and mix well again. Shape into patties.

Place on the grill and grill for about 5 minutes on each side. Or heat a pan on medium heat with a little oil and fry the patties for 5 minutes on each side.

BRATWURST WITH ONION-BEER SAUCE

Ingredients for 2 portions

2	Sausages
2 large ones	Onion, cut into rings
200 ml	Malt beer
150 ml	Broth
1 teaspoon	Food starch
1 teaspoon	Tomato paste
Salt and pepper	
Something	Caraway seeds, optional
N.B	Oil or clarified butter for frying

Preparation

Total time about 25 minutes

Fry the sausages in a little oil or clarified butter from all sides and keep warm between two warmed plates.

First roast the tomato paste in the frying fat, then fry the onion rings light brown, add the broth and malt beer and mix for approx. 5 min. simmer gently. Tie the sauce with the cornstarch and season to taste.

Cut the sausages into bite-sized pieces and reheat in the sauce. U can also have boiled potatoes or mashed potatoes.

UNKELER BEER STEW

Ingredients for 4 portions

400 g	Shallot, small
4	Carrot
500 g	Celery root
1.2 kg	Beef goulash (small pieces)
500 ml	Beer, dark
250 g	Beans, green (possibly frozen)
2	Bay leaves, (whole)
5	Stems Thyme, (fresh)
2	Clove of garlic (or garlic paste)
3 teaspoon	Tomato paste
2 teaspoon	Flour
3 teaspoon	Oil
10	Peppercorns, black

1 pinch	Sugar
1 pinch	Salt
Something	Pepper, freshly ground (white)
Something	Paprika powder, (sweet)
1 liter	Beef broth
500 g	Potato

Preparation

Total time about 2 hours 30 minutes

Put onions in boiling water, bring to the boil briefly, drain, rinse cold and peel off.

Depending on the size, cut the onions in half, Peel, rinse and cut carrots, potatoes and celery into bite-size pieces.

Fry the meat in portions in hot oil in a roaster or saucepan over high heat. Season with salt, pepper and paprika powder and take out. Fry the onions, carrots and the celery and potatoes in the dripping fat.

Add the meat and tomato paste to the vegetables and fry briefly. Dust with flour and braise for about 2-3 minutes. Pour in half a liter of broth and a 3/4 bottle of beer, bring to the boil and stir well.

Rinse off thyme. Peel and roughly crush the garlic. Add thyme, garlic, bay leaves and peppercorns. Bring everything to a boil and cover and simmer over low heat for approx. 2 hours. Stir occasionally and try to see if the meat is almost good.

In the meantime, clean, rinse and halve the beans (cleaning and rinsing is of course not necessary for frozen beans). Add the beans after approx. 1 1/2 hours and simmer.

Remove the thyme stems. Simmer a stalk or two about 10 minutes before everything is cooked properly and remove before serving. Season the stew with salt, pepper and sugar.

The stew can also be made well in the Roman pot. Then please reduce the amount of liquid to about half. Prepare the meat and vegetables as described above to the point where it says: "Bring everything to a boil and cover and simmer over low heat for approx. 2 hours". Place completely in the previously watered Roman pot and simply place in the cold oven and let it cook for approx. 2 hours at 180 ° C.

A strong crust or farmer's bread goes well with it (if you want to).

BEER GARLIC CHICKEN

Ingredients for 2 portions

1	Chicken, approx. 1400 g
½ liter	Beer
10	Toes garlic
1 tbsp	Oil

Salt and pepper

1 teaspoon	Sour cream

Paprika powder

Preparation

Total time about 55 minutes

Wash the chicken and dry it inside and out. Salt and pepper inside and out and season with paprika.

Sear the chicken briefly on all sides in a little oil.

Line the bottom of a roaster tightly with the whole cloves of garlic and bed the chicken on it. Now pour the beer into the roaster.

Now put the whole thing in the oven at 175 ° C for 20 minutes.

Pour beer over the bird occasionally and turn it halfway through the cooking time until it is brown on all sides.

Season the stock with salt and pepper and peel off with a little sour cream or similar.

Salt potatoes and apple red cabbage taste best.

BRATWURST BRAISED IN BEER

Ingredients for 4 portions

4 pieces	Bratwurst (coarse)
1	Onion, (finely diced)
125 ml	Beer, (black or brown beer)
125 ml	Water
1	Carnation
1 disc	Lemons
¼	Bay leaf
2 Tea spoons	Flour
Salt, (about 1/3 tsp)	
Something	Worcester sauce
1 teaspoon	Mustard, medium hot

Preparation

Total time about 20 minutes

The sausages are fried in hot fat on all sides until they are crispy.

Then remove from the pan.

Let the onions turn slightly brown in fat. Deglaze with beer and water.

Add the quartered bay leaf, clove, lemon wedge, salt, mustard and Worcester sauce.

Bring everything to the boil briefly and then put the sausages back in the pan.

Braise the sausages on low heat and a closed pan for 15-20 minutes.

Then remove the bay leaf, the clove and the lemon wedge from the pan, put the sausages on a plate aside.

Lightly bind the sauce with flour that has been stirred into a little water.

Then serve with boiled potatoes and vegetables of your choice.

BRATWURST GOULASH WITH BEER

Ingredients for 2 portions

300 g	Pork sausage, rough
1	Onion
1	Garlic cloves
1 tbsp	Extra virgin olive oil, cold pressed
200 ml	Beer, light
1 teaspoon	Paprika powder, hot or sweet as you like
1 teaspoon	Tomato paste
1 branch	Rosemary or about 10 dried rosemary needles
Possibly	Water

Preparation

Total time about 1 hour

Chop 1 onion and 1 clove of garlic. Cut the sausages into bite-sized pieces.

Heat 1 tablespoon of olive oil in a saucepan and sauté the onion, garlic and sausage until everything has taken on some color. Dust 1 tsp paprika powder over them, briefly fry with them. Deglaze with 0.2 l of beer, add 1 teaspoon of tomato paste and a sprig of rosemary.

Salt and pepper and cover and simmer on low heat for about 40 minutes. Possibly add some water. Serve with polenta, mashed potatoes or white bread.

BRAISED MEAT WITH BEER

Ingredients for 6 portions

3 m	Onions
8 m	Carrots, once halved and once lengthways
1 tuber	Fennel
1 large	clove of garlic, sliced
3 stems	Parsley, roughly chopped
2½ kg	Roast beef (from the comb)
2 teaspoon	Mustard, spicy
1 teaspoon	Flour
100 ml	Beer

Salt and pepper

Preparation

Total time about 8 hours 15 minutes

Put the onion, carrots, fennel, garlic and parsley in the crock pot. Season with salt and pepper; Put the meat on the vegetables. Mix the mustard with the flour into a paste and brush the meat with it. Season well with salt and pepper and pour over the beer. Put the lid on and cook at "low" for about 8 hours.

Serve the roast with the vegetables

SPARE RIBS BASED

Ingredients for 4 portions

300 ml	Ketchup (Heinz)
2 Tea spoons	Horseradish, spicy
10 drops	Worcester sauce
20 drops	Tabasco
1 Msp	Chili pepper
2 Tea spoons	Celery salt
4	Garlic cloves
1 teaspoon	Onion powder
2 bottles	Beer, dark
	Grill spice
4 kg	Pork ribs

Preparation

Total time about 1 hour 5 minutes

Mix a sauce of ketchup, horseradish, Worcester sauce, Tabasco, chilli pepper, celery salt, 2 - 4 cloves of garlic and the onion powder. Add 1 bottle of beer and stir until smooth. Place in a saucepan and simmer gently for about 20 minutes, stirring well.

Cut the ribs into portions and cook in a mixture of salt water and the rest of the beer for about 20 minutes.

Rub the cooked ribs with barbecue seasoning and grill on both sides for 10 minutes on the charcoal grill until they are nice and brown. Finally brush with the sauce and grill until it is firm - this is very quick. Serve immediately.

CHICKEN IN PLUM BEER SAUCE

Ingredients for 4 portions

4	Chicken thighs, maybe more
500 ml	Beer, dark
200 g	Prune
300 g	Onions, diced
50 ml	Cream, possibly more
1	Apple, sour, peeled, diced
3 branch	Thyme
2	Bay leaves
Salt and pepper	
3 teaspoon	Dijon mustard

Preparation

Total time about 1 hour

Soak the plums in the beer for at least 2 hours. Salt and pepper the chicken legs, fry them in butter and keep them warm.

Then fry the onions cut into cubes. As soon as the onions are glassy, deglaze with the beer and plum mixture and bring to the boil briefly. Reduce the temperature so that it no longer boils and add the chicken legs, the apple cubes, the bay leaves, the thyme and some salt. Ideally, everything should be covered with liquid.

30 - 40 min. braise, it shouldn't boil. As soon as the chicken legs are cooked, remove the sprigs of thyme and bay leaves. Add the mustard and cream to the sauce and puree the sauce. Possibly bind with starch dissolved in water.

IRISH SHEPHERD'S PIE WITH BEER

Ingredients for 8 portions

5	Onions
6	Carrot
	Olive oil
600 g	Minced beef or lamb (organic)
8 toes	Garlic, very finely chopped
1 bunch	Rosemary, fresh, chopped up
1 bunch	Parsley, fresh, chopped
1 bunch	Mint, fresh, chopped
Salt and pepper	
Paprika powder	
1 pinch	Cinnamon powder
1 small Can	Kidney beans, almost without juice
3 teaspoon	Ketchup

4 teaspoon	Flour
250 ml	Vegetable broth
500 ml	Irish beer
450 g	Peas, young, frozen
2 kg	Potato's, floury
75 g	Butter
200 g	Cheddar cheese, freshly grated
2	Egg yolk, whisked
5 teaspoon	Milk
	Cayenne pepper

Preparation

Total time about 2 hours 25 minutes

The quantity is designed for 2 baking dishes.

Halve onions, fifth and cut into 3 mm thick pieces. Quarter the carrots lengthways and cut into 7 mm pieces. Place the onions and carrots in a hot pan with oil and braise until the onions are translucent but not browning.

Remove the vegetables from the pan. Heat them again and fry the mince with a little oil and chop them. When the meat turns brown, add the garlic and fry until the escaping liquid has evaporated. Possibly reduce the heat.

Wash and chop the herbs. Peel the potatoes, cut up larger potatoes and cook gently in plenty of salted water.

Add the steamed vegetables and herbs to the meat and season with salt, pepper, bell pepper and cinnamon. Add the kidney beans and stir in a good dash of ketchup, Approx. Cook for 10 minutes over medium heat. Sprinkle the flour over it, stir in and cook everything for about 7 minutes. Slowly add the broth and beer and cook for another 7 minutes until a creamy mixture is formed. Stir occasionally.

Remove the pan from the heat and mix in the frozen peas. Place the mixture in a lightly greased baking dish. Spread evenly and press flat.

Drain the potatoes, drain and put them back in the pot. Add butter and cheese and mash. Whisk the egg yolk with salt, pepper, cayenne pepper and a little milk and mix with the mashed potatoes. Use a spoon to carefully pour the puree onto the meat mass and distribute it evenly. Either form small hills or traditionally pull strips into them with a fork. Bake in a preheated oven at 180 ° C for 25 - 30 minutes until the puree becomes crisp in places.

CHICKEN BRAISED IN BEER AND ONION SAUCE

Ingredients for 6 portions

1 tbsp	Butter or oil
1 kg	Chicken thighs, (6 pieces or depending on size)
N.B	Salt
1.3 kg	Onions, yellow, cut into slices about 0.5 cm thick
1 teaspoon	Sugar (optional)
4	Bay leaves, (dried or fresh)
6 branch	Thyme, fresh (or 2-3 teaspoons dried)
2 Tea spoons	Salt, (or to taste)
2 teaspoon	Dijon mustard, (without seeds)
500 ml	Beer, dark, malty
250 ml	Chicken broth
N.B	Pepper, black, freshly ground

Preparation

Total time about 1 hour 50 minutes

Melt the butter in a large saucepan with a lid (or roaster) over medium heat.

Pat the chicken drumsticks dry with kitchen paper and place them skin-down in the butter. Lightly salt the meaty side. Now brown the mallets all around (both sides). Remove from the roasting pan and set aside in a bowl.

Pour out the fat from the roaster except for 2 tablespoons - but do not pour away the burnt-on brown residues on the bottom, they have the delicious taste! Fry / cook the onions slowly, stirring occasionally. They should turn gently brown - this takes about 15-20 minutes, depending on the type of onion.

Fry the onion slices over medium heat. If you like, you can add sugar - but onions already contain enough sweetness, we omit the sugar.

Now add the bay leaves, thyme, mustard, salt and beer to the onions. Stir everything well and scrape off everything fried on the bottom of the pot and mix well with the onion mixture.

Add the chicken thighs and the chicken broth and make them simmer.

Cover and simmer for 45 minutes. Then remove the lid and continue to simmer until the liquid is greatly reduced and the chicken meat almost falls off the bone. This should take between 45 and 60 minutes.

Season with salt and freshly ground black pepper

BEER MUSTARD SLICED

Ingredients For 2 portions

250 g	Meat for sliced meat (beef, lamb, pork or poultry)
100 g	Mushrooms
50 ml	Sour cream
1 teaspoon	Lemon juice
100 ml	Broth
1 teaspoon	Flour
1 m	Onion
300 ml	Beer
2 toes	Garlic
Oil	
2 teaspoon	mustard
Pepper	
Cumin	

Paprika powder

Oregano (better use thyme when using poultry)

Preparation

Total time about 13 hours

Cut the meat into strips. Mix the oil and mustard well, season with pepper, cumin, paprika and oregano or thyme. Peel the onion, cut it into coarse pieces and add half of it to the marinade. Either finely dice or press the garlic (amount to taste) and add to the marinade together with the strips of meat and stir everything well. Fill up with beer until everything is covered, mix well again and leave covered in the fridge overnight.

Remove the meat from the marinade, dab lightly and fry in heated oil. Dust with 1 tablespoon of flour and let it brown for a short time. Then deglaze with broth.

In the meantime, cut the mushrooms into slices and lightly roast them in the pan with the remaining onions. Add to the meat and stir in the sour cream, Season with a portion of the marinade and a dash of lemon juice. Simmer between 20 and 40 minutes, depending on the type of meat.

BEER - CHICKEN

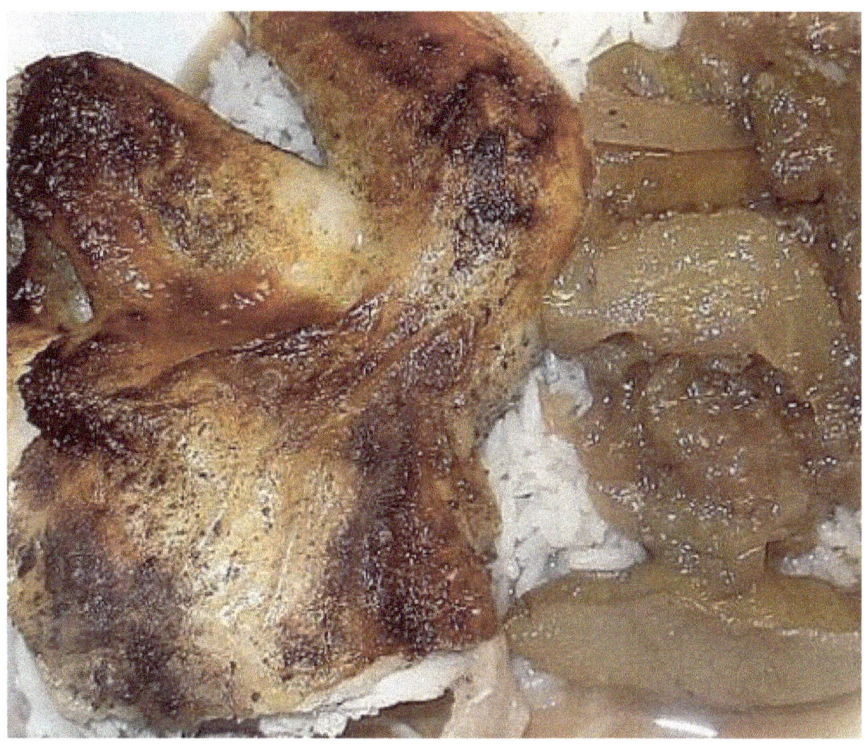

Ingredients for 6 portions

2	Chicken (1000 g each)
2 teaspoon	Oil (sunflower oil)
4	Apples
500 ml	Beer (pilsner)
4 teaspoon	Jelly (currant jelly)

Salt and pepper

Paprika powder, noble sweet

Preparation

Total time about 1hour 30 minutes

Season the chickens thoroughly with pepper, salt and paprika before cooking them in a roaster with a little oil at 180 degrees (top / bottom heat) in the oven for about 60 minutes. The chickens must always be poured with beer. Once they are crispy and clear juice comes out when you pee on them, take the chickens out of the oven and keep them warm.

To prepare the sauce, the washed, pitted apples must be cut into wedges and briefly steamed in the roast stock. Then add the rest of the beer and stir in the currant jelly, finally season with pepper and salt before serving the chicken halves with a little sauce.

MASTER BREWER'S DISH WITH BEER

Ingredients for 4 portions

500 g	Turkey breast or pork fillet
200 g	Chorizo or Cabanossi
1 teaspoon	Clarified butter for roasting
1	Onion
200 ml	Beer, dark
125 ml	Cream
125 ml	Chicken broth or vegetable broth
Something	Parsley, finely chopped
Something	salt and pepper

Preparation

Total time about 35 minutes

Cut the meat into strips about 2 cm thick, cut the sausage into slices about 0.5 cm thick. Finely dice the onion.

Heat the clarified butter in a pan, sauté the meat, sausage and onions all around. Deglaze with dark beer and cream and let everything boil down for about 5 minutes.

Now add the broth and season the sauce with salt and pepper. Allow everything to simmer until the desired consistency of the sauce is reached.

During this time, chop the parsley and sprinkle the parsley on the dish before serving.

BEER MUSTARD GRILL MARINADE

Ingredients for 2 portions

330 ml	Beer, your own favourite brand
1 large	Onion, finely diced
3 toes	Garlic, finely chopped
4 teaspoon	Mustard, spicy
1 bunch	Thyme, fresh, or 4 tbsp dried
2 teaspoon	Oil, neutral

Pepper, freshly ground

Preparation

Total time about 45 minutes

Heat the oil in a pan and lightly fry the onion and garlic, stir in the mustard and deglaze with 100 ml of beer. Remove from the heat, add the thyme, pepper and let cool. Then add the remaining beer and pour the marinade over the meat. Depending on the size of the meat, let it roast for a few hours, large roasts up to 2 days.

LENTIL SOUP WITH BEER AND BACON

Ingredients for 4 portions

250 g	Lentils, (plate lenses)
1 bottle	Dark beer (0.33 l)
1	Onion
1	Bay leaf
1 bunch	Soup vegetables
400 g	Potato
3 dice	Vegetable broth, instant
1 Can	Tomato, peeled (425 ml)
2 teaspoon	Vinegar
1.4 liters	Water, hot
Salt and pepper	
100 g	Bacon

Preparation

Total time about 4 hours 5 minutes

Soak the lentils in the beer for 3-4 hours. Cut the bacon into cubes and fry in a saucepan over medium heat. Cut the onion into cubes and add to the bacon and fry. Add the lentils with the beer, hot water and laurel. Bring to the boil and simmer for approx. 40 min.

Clean, wash and chop soup vegetables. Peel the potatoes and cut them into cubes. Add soup vegetables and potatoes to the lentils with the stock cubes about 10 minutes before the end of the cooking time. Drain the tomatoes, cut them into small pieces and add them to the soup. Season everything well with salt, pepper and vinegar.

BEEF SIRLOIN IN MUSTARD

Ingredients for 6 portions

3	Carrot
2	Onion
1 bar	Celery
750 g	Roast beef (beef sirloin)
Salt and pepper	
40 g	Clarified butter
200 ml	Water
1 branch	Rosemary
1 branch	Thyme
2 teaspoon	Mustard
200 ml	Beer (wheat beer or export)
1 teaspoon	Oil
250 g	Spaetzle

5 teaspoon	Puree (flake puree)
150 g	Crème fraiche Cheese

Preparation

Total time about 1 hour

Clean the carrots and cut them into strips, peel and dice the onions and celery. Pepper and salt beef loin. Heat the clarified butter in a roasting pan sear the beef loin vigorously on all sides for about 8 minutes. Remove from the roasting pan, boil the roast set with 50 ml of water, and stew the vegetables in the frying fat for 15 minutes. Add the remaining water, rosemary and thyme to the vegetables.

Brush the beef loin with mustard and put in the vegetables. Pour in the beer, braise in a closed pot in the oven (preheated) at 200 degrees for approx. 25 minutes. Bring salt water and 1 tablespoon of oil to a boil in a saucepan, cook the spaetzle bite-proof, drain and keep warm. At the end of the cooking time, remove the meat from the roasting pan, wrap in aluminum foil and let it rest for 5-10 minutes. Tie the sauce with mashed flakes add the crème fraîche, season with salt and pepper. Cut the beef loin into slices. Catch the meat juice, add it to the sauce arrange the meat with the sauce and spaetzle in an appetizing way.

ACHIMS BEER AND POTATO GRATIN

Ingredients for 8 portions

2 kg	Potato, firm cooking
250 g	Beef jerky or streaky bacon
200 g	Onion, diced
200 g	Chives, finely chopped
2 toes	Garlic
100 g	Mushrooms
1 teaspoon	Caraway powder
1 bottle	Wheat beer, light, 0.5
2 cups	Cream
200 g	Cheese (Gouda), young
1 teaspoon	Sunflower oil
5	Eggs

Breadcrumbs, for shape and for sprinkling

3 teaspoon	Butter, for the mold

Flakes of butter

3 splashes	Magi

Pepper

Salt

Nutmeg

Preparation

Total time about 2 hours

Peel and slice the potatoes. Wash the chives, clean them and cut them into fine rings. Wash, clean and cut the mushrooms into small cubes. Grate the cheese finely. Cut the beef into fine cubes. Peel the onions and cut them into fine cubes. Peel the garlic and cut it into fine cubes.

Drain the jerky in a pan on a low heat until glassy with a tablespoon of oil. Then add the onions and fry them until they are glassy. Sweat the garlic briefly. Add the beer, first 3/4, then shake so that the yeast comes off the bottom of the bottle and add the rest.

Mix 3/4 of the cheese with the cream and the eggs in a blender and season.

Place the bacon mixture with the potato slices in a large bowl and mix well. Then add the mushrooms, the chives and the egg mixture. Mix, season again and season if necessary. Then let it steep for approx. 15 minutes.

Butter an oval refractory form, sprinkle with breadcrumbs and pour everything in. Sprinkle on top with a mixture of breadcrumbs, butter flakes and cheese and bake in a preheated oven at 165 ° C for about 1 hour. When a golden yellow crust has formed on top, the gratin is ready.

A breaded cutlet or coarse bratwurst and a cold top-fermented beer go well with it. Asparagus and a beef steak are also good companions.

BRAISED PORK GOULASH WITH BEER

Ingredients for 4 portions

400 g	Pork neck, diced
400 g	Kasseler, diced
250 g	Onion
1 toe	Garlic, chopped
2	Carrots, peeled
3 teaspoon	Oil
Pepper White	
¼ liter	Beer, light
1 teaspoon	Basil, dried
1 teaspoon	Sage, dried
1 small can	Tomato, peeled, roughly chopped
2	Apples, sour, peeled, pitted, thick slices
Possibly	Salt

Preparation

Total time about 30 minutes

Put the can of tomatoes through a sieve. Catch the juice.

Heat the oil in a casserole. Fry the meat cubes in portions. Put the meat back in the pot. Add onions and garlic, season with pepper and sauté for about 5 - 10 minutes. Pour in the beer and tomato juice. Add carrots, basil and sage. Bring everything to the boil once and then cover and braise for 1 hour. Put the tomatoes and apple slices in the saucepan about 15 minutes before the end of the cooking time and sauté. Take out the carrots and dice very finely, add again. Season the goulash with pepper and possibly salt.

Strong bread, boiled or boiled potatoes also taste good.

CUCUMBERS IN BEER

Ingredients for 2 portions

1 large	Salad cucumber, about 800 g
Something	Salt water, boiling
1	Lemon, organic
375 ml	Beer, dark
2 Tea spoons	Sugar
1 teaspoon	Salt
2 Msp	Canning aid

Preparation

Total time about 2 days 20 minutes

Peel the cucumber and cut off the ends. Halve the cucumber lengthways, remove the stones and then cut into strips. Put the cucumber strips in a little salt water, bring to a boil, bring to the boil once and then drain on a sieve.

Wash the lemon hot, dry, rub half of the peel. Halve lemon and squeeze half. Cut 2 slices from the second half of the lemon.

Bring the beer to the boil in a saucepan with lemon peel, juice, sugar and salt. Add the cucumber strips and simmer for about 5 minutes over low heat.

Remove the pan from the hob and stir in the preserving aid.

BEER PASTA SALAD

Ingredients for 4 portions

250 g	Tagliatelle
Salt water	
150 g	Mayonnaise
50 g	Peas (TK)
50 g	Carrot (TK)
1 bottle	Beer, light
1 shot	Cream
Something	Salt and pepper
	Lemon juice
	Parsley, smooth to garnish

Preparation

Total time about 20 minutes

Cook the pasta according to the package instructions, drain and let cool. Mix the mayonnaise, cream and beer and pour over the pasta. Fold in the peas and carrots and season with salt, pepper and lemon juice.

BRAISED CHICORY IN BEER

Ingredients for 4 portions

4	Chicory, cleaned, the bitter end cut out in a wedge shape
120 g	Butter
500 ml	Beer, light
1	Sugar cubes, or 1 teaspoon
1 tsp, heaped	Chicken broth, instant
3 teaspoon	Breadcrumbs
3 teaspoon	Gruyère cheese, grated
Salt	
Pepper	

Preparation

Total time about 40 minutes

Spread a casserole with 100g butter and put the chicory in it. Close the lid and cook for 3-4 minutes on each side at medium temperature until the vegetables start to brown. Pour on the beer, add the sugar and chicken broth, salt and pepper. Close the lid again and stew the vegetables for 20 minutes.

Take out the chicory and put in a baking dish. Boil the gravy in the roaster until it has a syrupy consistency.

Then pour the sauce over the chicory, sprinkle with the breadcrumbs and the cheese. Spread the rest of the butter in flakes. Put the baking dish shortly before serving in the oven preheated to 200 ° C and bake until the crust has a golden brown color. Then serve immediately.

BEER ROOT VEGETABLES

Ingredients for 2 portions

2	Carrots
1	Kohlrabi
½	Celery root
1	Onion, diced
1	Clove of garlic, diced
50 ml	Beer, up to 100 ml
150 ml	Cream
	Salt and pepper
	Caraway seed

Nutmeg

Clarified butter

Preparation

Total time about 50 minutes

Peel the carrots, kohlrabi and celery and cut them into 1 x 1 cm cubes. Cook in boiling water for about 10 minutes.

Meanwhile, melt some clarified butter in a high pan and sweat the diced onion and the clove of garlic. Add the pre-cooked vegetables and deglaze with beer. Add the cream and let it reduce for approx. 10 min., Season with the spices.

This goes very well with boiled potatoes and pikeperch, trout or boiled beef or roast pork.

BEEF HIP STEAK WITH ONION BEER SAUCE

Ingredients for 2 portions

2	Steaks (beef), hip steaks
2	Onions, red, cut into strips
Something	Flour
2 dl	Beer, e.g. Scottish malt beer

Caraway seed

Thyme, chopped

Salt

Pepper

Oil

Preparation

Total time about 30 minutes

Steam the onions in a little oil, then dust with flour. Add half of the beer and let it simmer, Season with caraway, thyme, salt and pepper. Add the rest of the beer and let it simmer a little more.

Fry the steaks in a separate pan in heated oil, arrange the sauce on top.

CHEESE BEER TART

Ingredients for 4 portions

350 g	Flour, (smoked flour)
1 teaspoon	Salt
½ cube	Yeast, about 20 g crumbled
2½ dl	Beer, naturally cloudy
2 teaspoon	Mustard, coarser
250 g	Cheese, mixed it should be a good processed cheese
3 bars	Spring onion
Little	Pepper

Preparation

Total time about 1 hour 40 minutes

Mix the flour, salt and yeast in a bowl. Pour in the beer knead everything into soft smooth dough.

Cover and let rise twice at room temperature for about 1 hour.

Divide the dough into 4 pieces, roll out with a little flour to approx. 2mm thick ovals. Place dough pieces on two trays lined with baking paper.

Coat the ovals with coarse-grained mustard. Spread the cheese on top (it should be a good processed cheese), place the spring onions with pepper.

Slide the tray into the lower part of the oven and bake at 220 degrees for 15 minutes.

BEER CHILLI

Ingredients for 4 portions

500 g	Minced meat
1 tube	Tomato paste
2 box	Kidney beans
1 can	Corn
1	Bell pepper, red
2	Chili pepper
1 bottle	Beer, (pilsner)
2	Onion
4 toes	Garlic
	Paprika powder, noble sweet
	Salt and pepper
	Cayenne pepper
Chili flakes	

Cinnamon powder

Cocoa powder

2   Bay leaves

           Oil

Preparation

Total time about 12 hours 50 minutes

Fry minced meat in a large saucepan with oil and then add the chopped onions and garlic. Then add tomato paste and the beer cover it and let simmer for about 10 minutes. Then add beans, corn and the finely chopped peppers and stir everything well. Finally add spices (caution with cinnamon and cocoa, preferably a little less and season if necessary), cut the chillies and cook for about 10 minutes (longer or shorter, depending on the hotness), take out the chillies and bay leaves after cooking.

To get the full taste, let it rest until the next day.

It is best served with baguette and a cold bottle of beer (what else?).

BEER POTATO GRATIN

Ingredients for 6 portions

2 kg	Potato
150 g	Bacon
150 g	Onion, diced
150 g	Leek, finely chopped
Something	Garlic
300 ml	Beer (wheat beer)
400 ml	Cream
4	Egg

Salt, Pepper

Nutmeg

Caraway seed

Breadcrumbs

Butter, in flakes

Preparation

Total time about 20 minutes

Cut the peeled potatoes into slices.

Fry the bacon cubes in a pan, add the onions until they are nice and glassy.

Mix the beer, cream and eggs together. Place the glazed bacon and onion filling in a large bowl with the potato slices, add the leek and egg mixture, season and mix well.

Put the whole thing in a buttered gratin dish and sprinkle with breadcrumbs. Distribute the butter flakes evenly and bake in the oven at 165 ° C for about 1 hour.

VEGAN GOULASH WITH BEER

Ingredients for 3 portions

300 g	Meat substitute (veggie beef fillets)
4 m. In size	Onion
400 ml	Beer (pilsner or dark), or alternatively broth
500 g	Tomatoes, happened
1 teaspoon	Sugar
2 tbsp, heaped	Tomato paste
2 Tea spoons	Mustard, medium hot
2 teaspoon	Paprika powder, noble sweet
2 toes	Garlic
1 tsp, heaped	Marjoram
½ teaspoon	Caraway seed
1½ teaspoon	Salt
1 teaspoon	Lemon zest, grated

Oil for frying

Preparation

Total time about 1 hour 55 minutes

Sear the veggie beef fillets in portions in oil (highest setting). Add the diced onions and the sugar and reduce the heat a little. Let everything fry a bit, the onions are also welcome to get a few roasted flavors.

Then add the tomato paste and fry briefly then do the same with the paprika powder. Finally add the mustard and mix. Deglaze with the beer immediately in sips and wait briefly until it becomes a little viscous. Then slowly pour in the tomatoes and reduce the heat.

In a mortar, mix the finely diced garlic with the marjoram, cumin, salt and lemon zest to a paste and add. If you don't have a mortar, add the ingredients one by one.

Finally cover the goulash and stew on low heat for at least an hour, stirring occasionally.

Rice, noodles or potatoes go well with this.

SPARE RIBS WITH BEER

Ingredients for 4 portions

2 kg	Ribs
2 teaspoon	Oil
2 teaspoon	Chili sauce
2 teaspoon	Soy sauce
2 teaspoon	Honey
1 teaspoon	Mustard
1 bottle	Bock beer, or black beer
1 teaspoon	Chili powder
1 teaspoon	Curry powder
1 teaspoon	Paprika powder
N.B	Herbs, Italian, dried

Preparation

Total time about 6 hours 45 minutes

Cut the ribs into pieces. The best way to grill is with 2 to 3 ribs per piece.

Mix the oil, chilli and soy sauce, honey and mustard and season with the spices.

Brush the ribs with the marinade and leave them covered in a large bowl for at least 2 hours in the fridge, better overnight.

Then fill up with the beer. To keep the marinade on the ribs, put an inverted plate on the ribs and slowly pour the beer onto the middle of the plate. So it slowly runs into the bowl. Let it rest in the fridge for another 3-4 hours.

With the grill closed, grill at a low temperature until crispy brown. Turn occasionally.

For the open charcoal grill, I pre-cook the ribs on a tray with the complete marinade at about 170 degrees in the oven for 30-40 minutes. Then you can grill the ribs on the grill at normal to high temperature until they are crispy.

BREWERY GOULASH

Ingredients for 4 portions

500 g	Pork goulash
2 teaspoon	Clarified butter
½ teaspoon	Mustard
1 teaspoon	Tomato paste
1 large	Onion, chopped
1	Clove of garlic, pressed
1	Carrot, grated
200 ml	Beer, variety as desired
600 ml	Vegetable broth
Salt and pepper	
1 teaspoon	Paprika powder, noble sweet
1 teaspoon	Creme fraiche Cheese
N.B	Sauce binders

Preparation

Total time about 1 hour 35 minutes

Heat the clarified butter in a deep pan. Sear the goulash in the clarified butter and season with salt, pepper and paprika powder.

When the meat has a nice color and the water has evaporated, add the chopped onion, the pressed clove of garlic and the grated carrot as well as the mustard and tomato paste and continue to fry briefly.

Then deglaze with the beer and let it boil down. Fill up with the vegetable broth and simmer with the lid for approx. 1 hour (approx. 35 min when using a pressure cooker).

About 5 min. stir in the crème fraîche before the end of the cooking time and thicken with a little sauce binding agent if necessary.

Spaetzle, rice, mashed potatoes or boiled potatoes are suitable as a side dish

FLETCHER'S BEER ROASTER

Ingredients for 4 portions

1 kg	Beef, from the top shell or hip
8 disc	Bacon, streaky (beef jerky), not cut too thin
3 bottles	Beer, light (Kölsch)
4	Onions
3 toes	Garlic
250 g	Mushrooms, or mixed mushrooms
3	Bell peppers
3 branch	Lovage
2	Bay leaves
1 branch	Tarragon
2 teaspoon	Culinesse, or clarified butter
5 teaspoon	Flour
1 shot	Rice vinegar

1 tsp, heaped	Paprika powder, hot (alternatively chilli is also possible)
	Pepper, black, from the mill
Salt	

Preparation

Total time about 2 hours 30 minutes

Cut the meat into 2-3 cm cubes. Peel the onions and cut them into rings. Peel the garlic and cut into small cubes. Clean the mushrooms and cut them into medium-sized pieces. Wash the basil, lovage and tarragon, shake dry, pluck from the stem and chop. Put aside. Cut the beef into thin strips.

Make the Rama hot in a large frying pan and fry the meat cubes in portions. Transfer to a large roaster. Put the beef, cut into strips, with a little rama in the pan, leave on, the bacon should look a little glassy, add the onions and let them also become glassy. Now swivel the knob briefly, now add everything together to the meat.

Put a good shot of beer in the pan and stir until the roast has dissolved. Now pour the broth into the meat and stir everything well. Dust the flour over it, add the spices and herbs, stir vigorously and pour so much beer over it that everything is well covered.

Cover and simmer for 2 hours in an oven at 160 ° C. Maybe some beer needs to be refilled in between. Season again before serving and add the vinegar.

VEGAN COFFEE COCOA BEER CHILLI

Ingredients for 6 portions

250 g	Soybean granules, coarse
10 teaspoon	Soy sauce
5 teaspoon	Vegetable broth
3	Onion
3	Garlic cloves
1 pack	Tomato (s) happened
1 small Can	Tomato paste
1 glass	Tomato, dried, pickled in oil
250 ml	Beer, dark
100 ml	Espresso
2 teaspoon	Sugar, brown
1½ teaspoon	Cocoa powder
½	Oregano

½ teaspoon	Marjoram
3	Chili pepper
2 box	Kidney beans, poured
1 can	Corn, poured
	Pepper
	Cayenne pepper
	Nutmeg
	Paprika powder
	Some Oil

Preparation

Total time about 3 hours

Put the soy pieces in a large bowl and mix well with the soy sauce and the vegetable broth. Then pour boiling water over it. The bowl should be at least 3/4 full so that the soy pieces can open properly. Let it steep until the soy pieces have the consistency of fried minced meat.

Dice the onion, chop the garlic, cut the dried tomatoes into small strips, prepare the espresso, cut the chili peppers very small.

Braise onions and garlic in a little oil until the onions become translucent. Add the chili peppers and steam briefly. Add the passed tomatoes, tomato paste, espresso, beer, cocoa powder, herbs and bring to the boil briefly.

Drain the liquid from the soy pieces. The less you like salty, the better the soy sauce should be poured off possibly express the soy pieces a little.

Put the pieces of soy, beans, dried tomato and corn in the tomato sauce. If the chilli is now too thick, add water until the mix is right, season with other spices such as cayenne pepper, bell pepper, nutmeg, pepper. The chili should be salty enough with soy sauce and vegetable broth.

Let the chilli simmer on a low setting for about half an hour.

The longer it goes on, the tastier it gets, but you can also eat it straight away.

ROAST BEEF WITH BEER

Ingredients for 4 portions

500 g	Beef
1	Onion
1	Carrot
1 bottle	Malt beer
1 pack	Sauce cake (gingerbread)

Salt and pepper

Sugar

Vinegar

Oil

Preparation

Total time about 15 minutes

Season the meat with salt and pepper and fry on all sides in the oil. Add the chopped carrot and the chopped onion and sweat with deglaze everything with beer. Braise the meat until it is tender, add a little water if necessary.

Then remove the meat from the sauce, crumble the sauce pepper cake and let it boil in the sauce, season spicy with salt, pepper, sugar and vinegar. Either push the sauce through a sieve or puree with a blender.

Put the meat back in the sauce and serve with dumplings and red cabbage.

DESSERTS

BEER CREAM SLICES

Ingredients for 2 portions

2 pack	Puff pastry, frozen
300 ml	Milk
1 pack	Custard powder
2 teaspoon	Sugar
100 ml	Beer, dark or malt beer
200 g	Sour cream
150 g	Powdered sugar

Preparation

Total time about 2 hours 40 minutes

Preheat the oven to 220 ° C (fan oven 200 ° C). Cut each puff pastry sheet into 16 pieces (approx. 7 x 6 cm each). Place the pieces on two baking sheets covered with baking paper and bake in the hot oven for 10 - 12 minutes. Remove from oven and allow to cool.

Boil the milk for the beer cream. In the meantime, mix the pudding powder with the sugar and some milk. Add this mixture to the boiled milk while stirring, bring to the boil again and mix in the beer. Allow the pudding to cool a little, and then stir in a smooth mixture with sour cream.

Mix the icing out of icing sugar and beer. Halve the cooled puff pastry pieces lengthways. Brush the top halves with icing. Spread 1-2 tablespoons of beer cream on each of the lower halves and top with the tops. Let it harden in the fridge for at least 2 hours.

Tip:

For the beer pudding cream, stir the beer into the hot pudding only after boiling. This is the best way to preserve the fine taste of the beer. Pour in the beer carefully, because the carbon dioxide foams when it is stirred into the hot liquid. However, this is important because the carbonic acid must escape so that the cream is nice and soft.

MINI BRIOCHES WITH BEER AND CARAMEL SAUCE

Ingredients for 12 portions

500 g	Flour
15 g	Yeast, fresh
150 g	Sugar
3 teaspoon	Milk, lukewarm
100 g	Butter
2	Egg
Salt	
500 ml	Beer, dark
100 ml	Cream
3	Egg s, including the egg yolk

Preparation

Total time about 1 hour

Sieve the flour into a bowl and press a well in the middle. Crumble the yeast in and mix with the sugar and lukewarm milk. Cover and let rise for 15 minutes. In the meantime, melt the butter in a small saucepan and add to the batter with the eggs and salt. Work through the kneading hooks of the hand mixer. Then knead the dough vigorously with your hands until it blisters. Preheat the oven to 200 degrees. Grease the tins. First form the dough into a roll, then divide into 12 pieces of approximately the same size. Form a table tennis ball and a cherry-sized ball from each piece. First put the big ball in the mold then put the small one on it. Place the tins on a tray and let them rise for another 10 minutes. Meanwhile, melt the sugar in a saucepan for the sauce, Deglaze with the beer and reduce by half. Stir in the cream and reduce by a third, then let cool. Whisk the egg yolks, brush the brioches with them and bake in the middle of the oven for 15-20 minutes. Let the brioches cool a little and take them out of the tins. Sprinkle with sugar and serve with the sauce.

BEER - ICE CREAM

Ingredients for 2 portions

1	Egg yolk
100 g	Sugar
1 cup	Cream (half cream)
1 cup	Beer

Preparation

Total time about 20 minutes

Mix egg yolk and sugar until frothy in the blender. Mix the half cream and beer well and then mix with the egg yolk and sugar mixture.

The whole mixture then into the bain-marie (water bath) for 8 to 10 minutes!

Fill in glasses and place in the freezer.

MORE BOOKS FROM LACHLAN ANDERSON

Coorie Cooking: Scottish Recipes To Warm Your Heart And Heal Your Soul

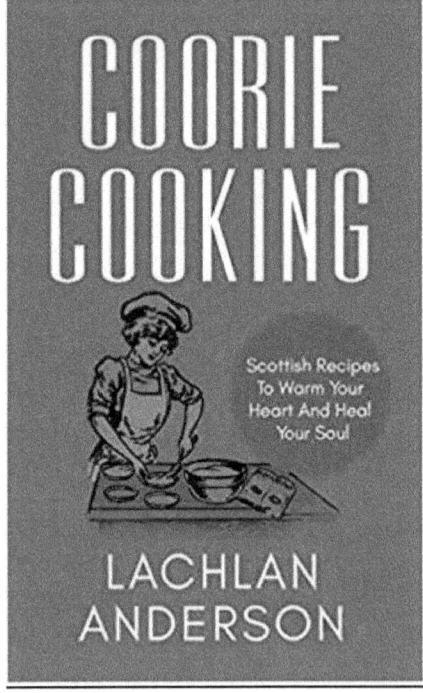

Coorie: What You Need to Know About The Scottish Lifestyle Trend

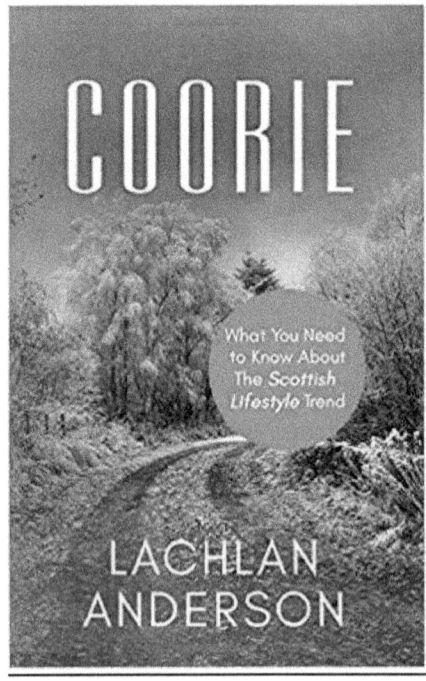

The Coorie Adult Coloring Book

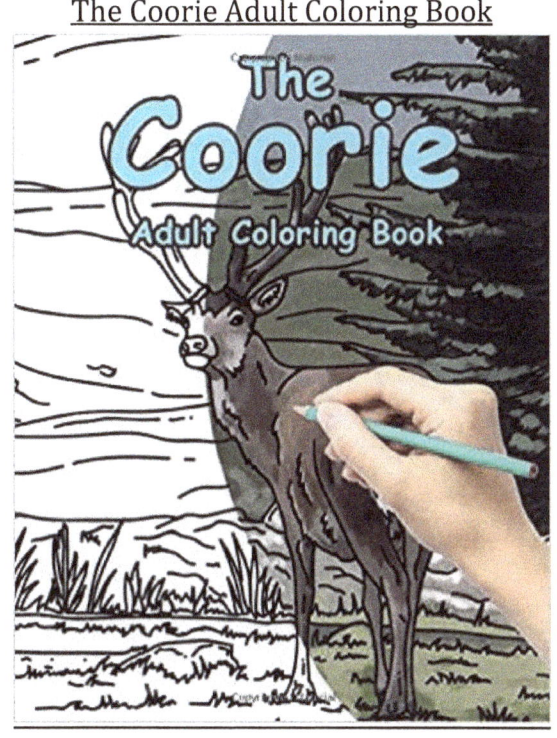

TO FINISH ...

I hope you enjoyed these recipes and had a great lunch or dinner with some of them! Thank you for buying this book and trusting my cooking.

I have invested a lot of evenings in putting together all these recipes and creating this great book. If you did me the favour of writing a short review on amazon or wherever you bought the book and have access to review it, this would make me extremely happy! Readers often underestimate the value their reviews have. In addition, as for me, I read every review, as it helps me to write better books in the future.

So thank you very much and ... enjoy your meal!